# Sex Magic

## HOW TO USE SEXUAL ENERGY TO MANIFEST YOUR DREAMS

## BY: LIZ PETERSON

### Raise The Vibe Books

**RAISE**
THE VIBE
BOOKS

**Also, by Liz Peterson:**

*"Mom Died Last Night*

*My shared death experience".*

*A memoir of death, grief, and afterlife*

*communication*

First Printing: 2024

eBook- ISBN: 979-8-9870619-3-0

Paperback- ISBN: 979-8-9870619-2-3

Library of Congress Control Number: 2024901835

Comments and inquiries regarding this book may be sent to the author: www.raisethevibewithliz.com

For updates and information, please follow-on social media:

@raisethevibewithliz

Published by Liz Peterson /

Raise The Vibe Books, LLC.

Vashon, WA 98070

Editing: David Zarate

Book Layout and Design: Liz Peterson

Cover Art: Shutterstock

Book Cover Design: Pasindu Lakshan (Fiverr)

Back Cover Photo: Rick Dahms

# **Contents**

INTRODUCTION .................................................xi

CHAPTER ONE
*What is Sex Magic?* ...........................*13*

CHAPTER TWO
*What is Manifestation?* ......................*21*

CHAPTER THREE
*Know your Energetic System* ...........*25*

CHAPTER FOUR
*Soul Integration* ...............................*41*

CHAPTER FIVE
*Grounding* ........................................*45*

CHAPTER SIX
*Intention* ...........................................*53*

CHAPTER SEVEN
*Setting up Sacred Space* ...................*59*

CHAPTER EIGHT

    *Protection* ........................................... 63

CHAPTER NINE

    *Sex Magic Practice* .............................67

CHAPTER TEN

    *Astral Sex* ............................................73

CHAPTER ELEVEN

    *Daily Pleasure Practice* ......................79

CHAPTER TWELVE

    *Let's Get Witchy* ................................. 83

About the Author ............................................ 87

# **<u>DEDICATION</u>**

This book is dedicated to
all you divine alchemists and
lovers out there.

# INTRODUCTION

Hello and welcome to your beautiful journey into the practice of Sex Magic: the tradition of using your lifeforce energy to create and manifest your most abundant life. For those of you that are new to me, my name is Liz Peterson. I'm an Author, Intuitive Energy Healer, Seer-Oracle, and podcaster - by way of Polarity Therapy, Core Shamanism and a 4-year energy work program focusing on Barbara Brennan's work (Core energetics, Shadow work, Somatic healing, and Reiki Master certification). I also personally work with Meditation, Tantra, Sacred Sexuality, and Yoni Shakti Womb Yoga in addition to hosting a podcast called Raise the Vibe with Liz.

I'm super excited that you've found your way to this book and begun your journey into working with this amazing manifestation technique. This is a favorite topic of mine since it landed into my life in 2018 via a channeled message during one of my own personal sexual experiences. I'll be sharing that download later in the book. Soon after I was guided to sex magic, the divine feminine, and Mary Magdalene from friends sharing their newfound knowledge of Tom Kenyon's book on Mary Magdalene's channel called, "The Magdalen Manuscript". The universe really wanted me to get this information... literally gifting me two of that very book!!

I found after reading the book, The Magdalen Manuscript, and my introduction into Tantra (as well as Sacred Sexuality via another acquaintance) shortly thereafter, that I'd been doing all of this work already... minus a full understanding of the role sexual energy / kundalini life force played. I'd been doing the energy work, the spiritual work, the meditations, and working with my kundalini energy since the late 90's - I just hadn't fully connected my sexual energy, aka lifeforce energy, as a tool for manifestation and liberation to the equation. I would learn this was the missing piece to living a life in not only ecstatic bliss, but full surrender to the natural divine flow of co-creation with both the universe and the divine. A life full of abundance!

# CHAPTER ONE

# What is Sex Magic?

I'm so excited this information is becoming more available and hitting mainstream media, television, and in magazines. I've seen it on Goop by Gwyneth Paltrow (go Gwyneth!), Netflix and Vice, social media, and books. There was even an article in Teen Magazine... Wow! Still, even though it's going mainstream I know the words sex and magic are often triggering for people. Ooh! SEX and MAGIC! But please keep an open mind. This is life changing! Not to mention it can be traced back to many areas of the world.

The dictionary says magic is, "The power of apparently influencing the course of events by using mysterious or supernatural forces." Yes. And... the magic that I am referring to is you! Your ability to have access to, and use, your inherent given energies to influence your life. With sex magic, magic is the alchemy of your vital lifeforce energy (!!) with alchemy being the magical process of transformation and creation.

Sexual energy is life energy. Its nature is to create. To not only create life, it can also be used to create YOUR life since both energies, creativity and sexuality, live in the same area of the body - the lower abdomen (2nd Chakra). So, it can be channeled to give birth as well as channeled to birth something you want to manifest into the world. Sexual energy naturally lifts your body into a higher vibrational state which can then be used to create meaningful change in your life.

In Tantra and the Sex Magic of Isis, sexual energies are used for the attainment of higher consciousness. Tom Kenyon and Judi Sion state via Mary Magdalene's channel, "The Sex Magic of Isis is precisely a method for the elevation of consciousness, which is, in itself, magic --- and this is done through the energies and ecstasy created through sex."

The use of sexual energy for transmutation has been used worldwide in a variety of ways and throughout time. Sex magic was an important part of Celtic spirituality practice, which is part of my ancestry. They aimed to deliver a spell by harnessing the energy of orgasms. "Druids believed that individuals could influence reality by focusing their own internal sexual energy", says John G. Hughes.

Pascal Beverly Randolph, an eclectic physician, created a sex magic practice based on the energy transfer between couples during sex. It was part of the OTO, Ordo Templi Orientis, a German magic order he founded in the 1890's. After which Alistair Crawley (a former member of the hermetic order of the Golden Dawn) was inducted into the OTO, and later positioned as head of the British section post studying and sharing the sex magic process during a visit to Egypt in 1909.

In Neo Tantra (the contemporary and western way of conceiving Tantra) or Sacred Sexuality, people practice the weaving together of spirituality and sexuality to reach higher states of being and evolution of the self. In Isis Temple Arts conveyed in a Mary Magdalene channel channeled by Tom Kenyon, Mary charged Yeshua's body - his KA body or energy body - via sacred union / sexuality so he could, "face the realms of death with greater power." Centuries ago in Tibetan Buddhism, monks invoked deities called Tantrikas to help charge their life force for liberation and awakening.

The ability to create our most abundant joyful life is in our nature and it is our birthright. We are born to be able to do it. Society, church and state, and the various limitations imposed on us over the years keep us blocked / shut down from experiencing our full sexual potential. This causes the majority of people to have shame and guilt around their sexual nature, but in truth it is one of your direct paths to finding God and communing with the divine. Some often have cosmic experiences while practicing sacred sexuality. And it can become a journey into self-realization; the knowledge to "know thyself" is to know that you are a God spark - God incarnate. In spiritualism we are a fractal of consciousness - the "all that is". We are oneness, God / consciousness incarnate realizing itself as us.

It is my hope that by bringing this practice into the larger discussion - and normalizing it - that it becomes a way forward to not only help us to reclaim our personal power, but reclaim this powerful tool that we should all be taught and practicing. It could literally change the world!

You see, your sexual energy is a source of power that can be channeled into a goal, desire, or vision which can be realized by raising your sexual energy via self-pleasure or consensual partnership. The act of Sex Magic is using our orgasm, or orgasmic energy, to manifest. Energetic or magnetic fields are created by the stimulation of arousal states in the body. As we build these states we charge and increase our energetic field and the energy created may be used for alchemy (transmutation). It's the cultivation of our lifeforce energy, our Chi (Ki), by consciously moving energy through our bodies via our energetic system. We are bringing our body, mind, and spirit into a collaborative focus. We use our orgasmic electric field to awaken our creator potential to create (or co-create) the life we desire.

We use our life force energy to back or fuel our intentions, our desires, and then we release those intentions or desires to the universe - thus releasing them to the divine to handle the outcome. This outcome is always grander than we could imagine and often better for us. Our intentions are prayers, our hearts desires sent out into the cosmos for realization.

In magic, the orgasm is considered the ultimate magical force. Through sacred sex, we can use our sexual energy, our eros, not only for pleasure but to transmute, to alchemize, and to manifest our reality. It's charging our energy system with this eros and infuses the intention we want to manifest with this energy, allowing the orgasmic energetic power to enhance our manifestation practices. Then we release our intention we desire to manifest into the ethers, surrendering it to a higher power to do the rest.

Tantra is a spiritual discipline that outlines a path to enlightenment. Tantra means to weave together or to compose. In the Indian tradition it is regarded as books or texts that describe practices to reach the divine. It's a way to weave together the physical and the spiritual. It's all about embodiment and living through the body.

In some Tantric practices we are taught to harness the physical body and our sexuality in order to unite with divinity and attain transformational power: teaching direct engagement with sexual energy. To seek enlightenment and commune with the divine as a path to liberation.

Sex magic is taking transformational sexual energy and using it toward the betterment of our lives. It often ends up transcending the actual sex act itself, filtering into our entire life's experience. The gifts from practicing sacred sexuality gives us a sense of joy, bliss and mindfulness. When you're working with your lifeforce energy / triggering your kundalini energy everything in your life will naturally become more joyful, and all your senses will be heightened. This joyful way of being not only trickles into our entire lives, but the lives we connect with and into the collective consciousness. Because what we do personally affects the whole of humanity. As within, so without!

We can do the sex magic practice with a consensual partner in sacred relationship, or solo during our self-pleasure practice. If you are having sex or working with your eros (pleasure / sexual self), you can have a sex magic practice! It's only a shift in intention.

# CHAPTER TWO

# What is Manifestation?

Everyone everywhere is talking about manifestation or the law of attraction these days. And not just individuals. People are discussing it for themselves, in business, and it seems everyone in the spiritual communities are either posting about it or offering classes on it. Remember the movie The Secret? The book sold more than 30 million copies.

For me manifestation is having a relationship with and being in co-creation with the universe. It's listening to my intuition and knowing that I am one with the universe and a powerful co-creator with all of nature as the universe.

Manifestation is an act or process of creating or bringing into reality your dreams, visions, desires and goals or visualizing success and positive outcomes. You can choose to try to manifest anything into your life.

Some ways in which I've manifested in my life are affirmations, gratitude, positive thinking, visualization, vision boards and sex magic.

I've used positive affirmations when attempting to change an emotion, limiting belief, or heal trauma. I've practiced gratitude throughout my life when trying to stay positive or bring more happiness and joy into my life, in addition to walking myself through grief and pain. I've used visualization during my meditation practices. And I've done vision boards every year to call forth my desired years' experience.

Over the last few years, I've noticed that thoughts and words that have been spoken quickly turn into reality. It's a product of our shifting times and consciousness. If you are stepping into a flow with the universe, you will experience instant manifestation. It's just a matter of allowing yourself to follow your intuition and have awareness of your inner and outer experience.

It takes patience when trying to invoke your will to manifest something outside of divine timing. It may not happen right away because the universe must orchestrate what you desire. However, I have manifested many things into my life. These include a radio show, my podcast, homes, money, travel, and love - I've seen it happen over and over again. All it takes is a vision, a thought, and your energy. If you can dream it, you can manifest it!

# CHAPTER THREE

## Know your Energetic System

To learn sex magic, we need to understand our energetic foundation. First let's dive into our energy system and what it consists of... because sex magic is about moving our energy, our

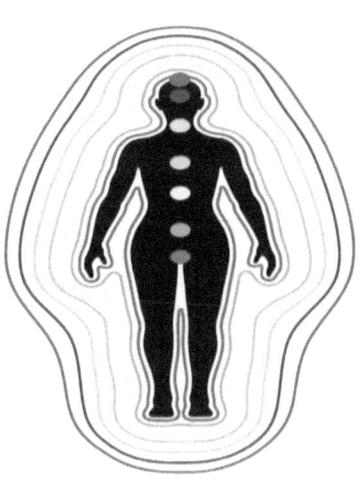

lifeforce energy. And that energy mastery resides in our energetic system.

Our energetic system is comprised of the Aura, Chakras, and Central Channel otherwise known as the Hara or Shashumna in Sanskrit, Died in Egyptian.

The information I will be sharing is what I have learned and practiced over the last 30 years. It is based on the basic 7 major chakra system practiced in western society, and not from a classical tantra tradition / lineage.

## The Aura

We are energetic beings and have an electricity about us. The Aura is a luminous energy field or electro-magnetic field that surrounds and emanates from a living being. Even plants, trees, and animals have an aura. After absorbing energy, objects can emanate an aura too. The scientific term for the Aura is Biofield.

There are seven layers of the Aura that radiate out from the body. Each layer correlates to a different aspect of the physical, emotional, spiritual, and mental self. They are simply referred to as the first, second, third, fourth, fifth, sixth and seventh layers of the field... or the physical, emotional, mental, astral, etheric, celestial, and katheric (spiritual), layers of the field: with each layer holding a different vibration.

The odd layers of the field are solid or structured in nature, and even layers are like pastel clouds or unstructured in nature with the outer most part of the 7th layer being called the golden egg. The layers are 1 - blue, 2 - pastel clouds, 3 - yellow, 4 - pastel clouds, 5 - cobalt blue, 6 - brilliant light, and 7 - golden light.

As a whole, your Aura emanates it's own frequency. This vibration can be felt or sensed by others and sometimes even seen. Since it holds your emotions and energy, a person can either be attracted to or repelled by your aura. Those who can see and feel auras can find energetic thought forms, objects, tears, rips, holes, cords, illness, and much more in the field. It is a direct reflection of what is going on in the body. Each layer also corresponds to one of the Chakras. Chakra in Sanskrit means wheel of light and refers to energy points in the body / energetic body.

## Chakras

There are seven major Chakras in the physical body. Starting with the first Chakra at your perineum in the genital area. They are seated at designated energetic points up the central channel (hara) and end at the top of the head with the seventh Chakra. They are vortices of light shaped like a cone. The tip of that cone points inward toward the central channel - in the front and the back of the body. They have a clockwise spin and represent our seven layers of consciousness.

The first Chakra, or base Chakra, is red. This is the Muladhara Chakra in Sanskrit. It represents our grounding, stability, safety and survival - all things earthly. This Chakra is seated at the perineum and connects us down into the earth.

Our second Chakra, or Sacral Chakra, is orange. The Svadhisthana Chakra in Sanskrit is seated just below the naval – in the sacrum area. It represents our sensuality, sexuality, personal power, creativity and ability to manifest, create, and birth things into the world.

The solar plexus Chakra, our third chakra, is yellow. The Manipura Chakra in Sanskrit is seated at our solar plexus, right at the top of our stomach (abdomen) area. It represents strength, power, ego, feelings of self and other as well as family of origin.

The fourth chakra is the heart Chakra, the Anahata Chakra in Sanskrit, and it is green. It is the bridge between the lower and upper half of the body - the bridge between the physical and etheric plane. Located at the center of the chest and back... it represents love, compassion, acceptance, and peace. It is also the home of our clairsentience or clear feeling. When we're moving our energy up through our body during sex magic, we pass it through our heart chakra and up through the top of our head.

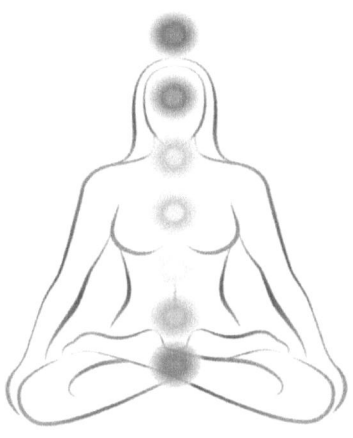

When practicing sacred sexuality, the heart plays a key role. When our sexual energy begins to flow, we can breathe this energy up into our heart on an inhale. Not only does it increase the energy flow, but it also increases and builds our Eros (sexual energy). When we are doing breathing exercises, we can circulate our energy via our breath to create a circuit of energy within us. When working with a partner we can create a circuit of energy that flows between us.

The fifth Chakra, located at the center of the throat, is our Throat Chakra... or Visuddha Chakra in Sanskrit. The color blue, this chakra represents communication, expression, and honesty. The throat Chakra is the home of psychic hearing (clairaudience), smell (clairalience) and taste (clairgustance). It's our voice and having a voice for ourselves - speaking up for ourselves - and having a voice in the world. It's also voicing our creation into the world. Making sound through our fifth Chakra triggers our Vagus nerve, which then triggers our nervous system to relax. When we make sound, hum, sing, or recite mantras, it can also trigger our pineal gland. Our fifth Chakra is also linked to our second Chakra, our seat of power; both pertain to our creative forces. No voice = no personal power = no self-empowerment.

Breathing circulates our energy, and making sound opens the body and releases energy and emotion. Breath and sound both open the body and move the energy throughout the body. I'll note here - if you are having trouble having an orgasm, make sound and breathe! It can help you reach orgasm. Try it!!

The sixth Chakra is called the third eye Chakra, or Ajna Chakra in Sanskrit. It is located between the brows and is the color indigo. It is our center of mystical intuition and insight. It is the Chakra of inner sight, intuition, visualization, inspiration, imagination, and psychic sight (clairvoyance).

The seventh Chakra or crown Chakra, Sahasrara in Sanskrit, is located at the top of the head. It's the Chakra which connects us to source – to creation – to the divine – and the galactic center. It is the Chakra of knowledge, fulfillment, spirituality, and self-realization. The color is white to white violet. It is the home of clear knowing (Claircognizance), the psychic ability of just knowing things.

# Central Channel

The final piece of the energetic system is the central channel or Hara (Shashumna in Sanskrit / Djed pillar in ancient Kemet / Egypt). The Hara is the core power source that resides beneath the Aura and that the Chakras align to. It's the Auras foundation. This is where your life purpose is located, the source of your creativity, and where your intentions are held and birthed. Your Hara line is a line that aligns vertically with your physical body, bottom to top, with three centers - the tan tien (belly), the heart, and the 3rd eye. If your hara is straight and aligned you will be in your integrity, power, and purpose!

shutterstock.com · 415342540

During sex magic this is the line our intentions travel on before being released to the cosmos. I also see the hara as the vagus nerve and the pathway of the kundalini energy. Kundalini is our lifeforce energy that begins coiled up at the base of our spine at the perineum, and when released goes all the way up through our central channel / hara to the top of our head. In eastern philosophy the kundalini is shown as two intertwining snakes (one black, one gold), called the Ida (left side -feminine) and Pingala (right side - masculine) that wind up the Shashumna (Hara) and intersect each of the Chakras as it travels to the crown of the head (as depicted in the Caduceus and the image above). It is said that once your kundalini is fully realized or "awakened", you achieve enlightenment, or are enlightened.

When kundalini is first activated it is often felt as arousal or sexual energy. Kundalini is a spiritually creative energy and in the physical it is creator energy. This is the energy that participates in creation which is why it plays a role in sex magic. One of my kundalini openings was a spontaneous and gentle kundalini awakening that occurred in 2018 while at the kitchen sink doing afternoon dishes. It came out of nowhere as repetitive waves of energy traveling up my core and was orgasmic!

As your sexual energy awakens in this way it can be beneficial to slowly awaken your kundalini by channeling that energy to ascend the spine. This can be done by running your energy with sacred sexuality, breathwork, meditation, and/or movement. Kundalini, when activated, can feel like warmth, fire, waves of energy and tingling in the feet, hands, and legs; it can have a sound as well like a rushing in the ears. Awakening of this kundalini energy can happen through practice or spontaneously in different ways and throughout your lifetime.

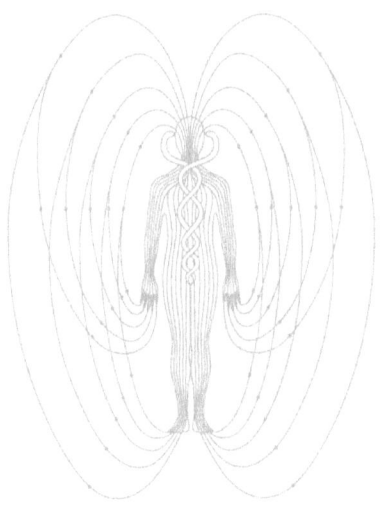

Our energy system mimics that of our planet. Just like our earth has a toroidal field, so do we. This toroidal field is what the energy looks like when it's circulating around the body as it mimics what the Earth does. This field can also be created in pairs.

I was at a local musicians' event one evening where there was a couple up on stage singing together and playing guitar. They had this type of beautiful aura around them up on stage in the shape of the toroidal field - the shape of a heart encasing the two of them. So, know that when you and a partner are together and you're feeling love, or in energetic resonance while making love, this aura is around you and you're moving the energy together just like the couple that I witnessed on stage.

## Breathing Exercise

To circulate sexual energy between two bodies... begin by one person inhaling their energy up from their genitals to their heart, then exhaling this energy from their heart into their partner's heart. The partner then breaths in this energy into their heart and sends it down into their genitals... circulating it back to the other person from their pelvis on the exhale. This creates / circulates a conduit of energy flowing through our bodies for heightened pleasure.

The person exhaling from their heart to their partners heart is known as the feminine breath (but can be practiced by both male and female embodied individuals). With the feminine breath you can add a "mmmm" sound (lips closed) to your exhale. The person exhaling from their genitals into their partners genitals is called the masculine breath. They use an "aaah" sound with their exhale, exhaling outward from the mouth.

This is a great exercise for learning how to move energy between you.

During the sexual manifestation process, we're moving the sexual energy through our bodies, pulling it up through our bodies and sending it out the top of our heads and into the ethers (more on this later). This breathing technique is really fun if you're in a position called Yab Yum together.

Yab Yum is when two people sit facing one another, one on top of the others lap. Traditionally it's performed with the woman on the man's lap, but you can mix it up! The top person is the feminine representation, and the bottom person will be the masculine representation.

## Energetic Sex

Come together with the person on top sitting on their partner's lap. Sit face to face with both of you in a cross - legged position (if comfortable), while looking into each other's eyes. This is a fun position to play with the divine masculine and divine feminine energy. The partner choosing the female embodied energy sits on top and practices the feminine breath. The partner choosing the masculine embodied energy sits on the bottom and uses the masculine breath. Playing around with the energies and switching roles allows us to experience our divine feminine energies and our divine masculine energies. All of us have both and can play, experiment, feel and experience what it's like to embody both the divine feminine and the divine masculine energy.

Yab Yum is a great position to practice energetic sex in. Energetic sex can also be done with the clothing on and without touch. Many people can experience sexual pleasure without actually having penetrative sex or physically touching themselves or being touched by a partner. When engaging in energetic sex, you can have lovely energetic orgasms or bring yourself to a hands-free orgasm. Anytime you feel pleasurable pulses passing through your body you are experiencing an energetic orgasm. They usually begin in the pelvis and move up the body like a wave. Enhancing this wave with inhalation can help to bring the energy up into your heart and body.

A simple energetic sex practice is to incorporate the breathing exercise above and add an expansion and contraction with your body that follows the breath. Arching your body on the inhale and rounding the body on the exhale. Similar to cat cow in yoga, or kundalini yoga breath exercise. By rocking the pelvis in this way, you trigger your sexual energy - or eros - to activate and move. Where you go from there is up to you (wink wink). ***This can also be done solo.

Our energy system works for us, through us, as us. For example - when we get channeled an idea through our seventh Chakra, we see and imagine it with our sixth chakra, voice it into the world via our fifth Chakra, feel into it via the fourth Chakra, run it through our family systems in the third Chakra, and then birth it into the world via our second Chakra, onto the planet via our first Chakra. They work together!

For sex magic we get embodied through our 1st Chakra and our sexual fire is lit in our 2nd Chakra. Then we channel it through our 3rd Chakra (feelings of self and other) up into our hearts (4th Chakra) where we fuel it with love, expressing ourselves through our 5th Chakra with breath, sound and creativity; visualizing our intention through our 6th Chakra, and then realizing ourselves, our intention, and communing with the divine through our crown - the 7th Chakra.

# CHAPTER FOUR

## Soul Integration

In 2018 I received a download from the universe about a missing piece of the sexual manifestation practice. Before I began my own practice that day, I was guided to call back any-and-all fractured off soul aspects of my sexual being back to myself to reintegrate.

Over our lifetimes, we've had different things happen to us that could have caused us trauma around our sex or sexuality. At these moments in time a part of ourselves can get stuck in that moment in time, either left behind or fractured off. We want to reintegrate these pieces of ourselves to come into wholeness since it's believed that one can be incomplete when this happens. In shamanic work there is a process called soul retrieval where we can find these fractured off pieces of ourselves and reintegrate them back into our present self for healing. It's through becoming a whole embodied person that we find our wholeness, personal power, and autonomy aka our strength. This process of reintegration and embodiment is not only healing, but it also amplifies your magic!

This is a very easy process, and all it takes is intention, incantation, and imagination. Like I said previously, our imagination is the gateway to reality. Intention is our ask. And an incantation is an invitation. I often say this simple incantation during my own solo or partnered sex magic practices--

"I ask that all sexual aspects of myself that have been fractured off from my being reintegrate back within me with ease and grace."

If you would like to do a separate practice beforehand, you can also do a shamanic practice with a practitioner, on your own, or with your partner. There are many drum journey recordings available for download. The process is simple, here's an example journey process.

## Journey Exercise

Find a comfortable, quiet place to lie down. Consider putting on an eye mask and set an intention that you are journeying to find your missing aspects. Begin by listening to the drum journey selection and follow the drumming down into your inner world to find the missing aspect or aspects of yourself. Next ask it or them if they would like to come home and reintegrate and if it's a yes, feel them reunite with you. When the drum track calls you back, come back into the present moment.

By adding this to our practice, we can work on healing those parts of ourselves that experienced the trauma and were fractured off along the way, from our past to present day. It can help us to feel more present, move past an issue, begin our healing process or know the root cause. It can also break old patterns, remove old energies, change limiting beliefs and understand ourselves. Furthermore, it can increase our vitality, give us an expanded sense of wholeness or wellbeing and help us feel more balanced and centered. Since this is in relation to our sexual history it also has the possibility to heal our sexuality and our present-day sexual experiences for the better. Because when we endeavor to heal our past wounds and traumas, we free ourselves up to living a more fulfilling life in all aspects of our lives, including our sex and sexuality.

# CHAPTER FIVE

# Grounding

When we're working with energy, we must learn how to ground. Grounding is plugging in or electrically reconnecting our energy into the planet and becoming embodied energetically within our physical bodies. This leaves your soul fully centered and aligned within the physical body and connected into the earth. A simple grounding process I use is to imagine roots coming out of the bottom of my feet and into the earth... or I send a cord out of the center of my body and connect it with the earth. Next I feel into my body and my energy body (soul) to make sure my energetic self is in my physical body and that I am aligned and centered.

You can also do this by putting your bare feet on the earth, sensing the cool or hot air around your skin, and deep breathing. Play around with this and use your imagination (remember, the imagination is the gateway to reality).

After I feel embodied, I imagine energy rising from the earth and into my body. We can then learn how to channel that energy up and down our spine, which is called running energy.

When we're doing sex magic it's good to have a feeling of being embodied and present, and to be able to feel the sensations of the energy moving up and down your body.

## Grounding Exercise

Here's a simple exercise to walk you through grounding and moving energy:

- Take a seat and put your feet on the floor. While your feet are planted on the floor (and sitting with an erect spine like you're going to be doing meditation) feel the ground rising to meet your feet.

- Close your eyes if you like and really feel your sit bones on the chair.

- Feel heavy in your seat and feel your feet sinking into the ground beneath you.

- Now feel your energy going down into the ground. Your body getting heavy, feeling your seat, the weight on your shoulders, and energies pressing upon your head.

- Take some time and breath into how this feels to be embodied and present.

For sex magic, we really want to have a sense of our body, have that feeling sense in our body, and know what's going on within our bodies as opposed to being dissociated.

Next feel down into the tip of your tailbone, and imagine a cord is reaching down into the earth from your tailbone.... all the way down into the earth!

Think of it like a tree's taproot. Send this chord all the way down into the earth and wrap it around a rock deep within the molten core that lies at the center.

Now sense if you have any of your energetic body outside of your physical body. If you're feeling you may be leaning to one side, or feel like you're kind of in your head, try to bring that energy into the center of your body. Like you're aligning that energy back into your core (center).

(My energy tends to be off to the right, so I consciously bring my energy body back into my center.)

Now inhale earth energy through the cord you've connected down into the earth and pull it up into your body.

Use your imagination to pull this energy from the earth into your body and into your first chakra at the seat of your spine. It is a vortex cone opening towards the Earth.

Bring it all the way up into that chakra and into your pelvis. Just let it be here and move around in this space. See if you can feel anything moving in your pelvis. Visualize the color red! Just have an awareness, take a breath, and feel. Breathing in can help pull it into your body.

With your next breath, pull the energy up to your second chakra, your navel, and have an awareness that it's at the second chakra. Visualize orange filling up your abdomen, and expanding into your belly.

As it travels through your stomach, it reaches your third chakra right at your solar plexus. While in the diaphragm area, picture yellow. Breath it in, expand it and pull that energy up from the earth.

Now let it rise up into your fourth chakra at your heart as you visualize green energy filling that area. Breathe it in deeply (you might start feeling full like your chest is expanding and your heart is opening!)

As your heart chakra starts to fill and expand, allow it to flow into your fifth chakra, while picturing blue, as it naturally moves up to your throat. As you feel it fill and open, you may want to take a deep breath and make a sighing sound to further open up the throat chakra. Maybe even yawn!

Next take a deep breath and feel the energy as you breathe it up from the earth and pass it through your first, second, third, fourth, and fifth chakras.

As it expands, you let it naturally move to your sixth Chakra, in-between your eyebrows. Take an inner gaze with your eyes to the center of your forehead, and just let that energy fill your head, having an awareness of it there and expanding.

Then letting that energy leave out the top of your head through the seventh chakra (which is a cone that is opened toward source) as it continues up towards the heavens, and connect to source.

As you connect above imagine pulling that energy back down through your seventh chakra and into your sixth chakra. Continue bringing it down to your fifth chakra at your throat, then into your heart. Take a deep breath.

Now send it down further into your belly and into your seat. All the way through the tip of your tailbone and into the ground.

Follow your breath. As you inhale, bring the energy through your body all the way to the top of your head.

Then on the exhale, allow the energy to sink back down into your lower belly.

Repeat this a few more times.

After a few rounds gently come back to the room, allowing your eyes to slowly open, your toes and fingers to slowly move, and perhaps even a nice stretch or two.

Then take a deep breath and just let it all go.

While working with our sexual energy during sex magic, we're going to be pulling that sexual energy up and shooting it out the seventh chakra for manifestation when we surrender it to source.

# CHAPTER SIX

# Intention

*What is intention and why do we want to set an intention?*

The dictionary says, "intention is a thing intended, an aim or plan." Intention is a voluntary direction of the course of one's thoughts toward a selected idea.

The reason we want to set intention is because this is how the magic really happens!

An intention is a wish that you want to carry out. It's having a goal to achieve something. It's a prayer to the universe, source, the divine, or creator (insert your preference here).

When you set an intention, you're using your internal focused attention to create the life you want. Intentions help us to achieve our goals, move us forward in our lives, and improve the quality of our lives.

When practicing sex magic, we must think deeply on what we want to manifest, what our desires are and then put thought into those intentions.

Again, in order for our intentions to be manifested, and to practice sex magic, we need to get clarity around our thoughts so we can be precise with our ask. It's worth stating twice!

Buddha says, "With our thoughts, we make our world." Where attention goes, our energy flows! So having a clearer idea of what we want to manifest I feel is very important. And we want to be specific because we're going to be infusing this intention with our directed sexual energy.

After we decide what we want to intend we will be thinking about it, seeing it, feeling it, envisioning it, and eventually sending it out to the cosmos. We want to be very clear about what we are going to manifest. We can channel and use our sexual energy to back anything - health, love, wealth, a project that you're working on, a vision, manifesting a house, for the betterment of your life or another's, the collective, or the planet. Whatever your heart desires!

I would suggest picking one thing to put your energy into to start. That way, you're not multitasking, and all of your focused energy can go into manifesting that one thing. You don't want to thin the energy so to speak. So, when you're setting intentions, each person can pick one thing that they want to intend (or you can have a shared vision together). If you're solo and self-pleasuring, you still have your set intention that you're putting out to the universe... or you can offer up someone else's as well.

## Intention Setting Exercise

**Step 1** - Get clear! What do you want to manifest?

**Step 2** - You want to write it down. Writing it down and saying it out loud really says to the universe, "this is what I want!" It engages the universe like a prayer. It's not just inside your head, it's an ask to the universe. You're putting in your order. Just like when you pray for something, you're saying it out loud (or may be writing it down) and putting it out to a higher power, saying "Hey, I am asking for help with this, and this is what it looks like."

After you've written it down and shared it, if you're with another person(s), you can put it on your altar (I'll be talking a little bit about that later). You can also slide it under your bed mattress or you can have it on the bedside table next to yourselves. But just write it down! That helps you get clear, it helps you to put the energy out there and begin the process.

**Step 3** - Next what you want to do is share the intentions with each other. Verbalizing your intentions puts your words out into the ethers. It affirms your ask to the universe. Your words have power! They are a prayer to the universe whether said aloud or in your head! So, you want to talk about your intention. You want to say what your intention is, what your desire is around this intention, what that looks and feels like to you so that you and your partner can really feel into and embody what you're intending.

Now would be a good time to share any limiting beliefs you may have around your intention with yourself or your partner(s). Because if you're having an intention, and you've got your inner voice saying it doesn't believe it's possible, you need to clear those beliefs.

For example, say you're trying to manifest more money. Money is a common ask - people want to manifest more money. But what if you have a limiting belief around money and see money as a limited resource. Lots of people have a variety of limiting beliefs (or negative beliefs) around money. Some of these could be "I'm too old, I'm not smart enough, I'm not educated enough, I try and I fail or I've tried everything. If I'm asking for money, that's selfish. Do I deserve it? Am I worthy? It's a limited resource. It's the root of all evil."

What were you programmed to think about money? What did you hear your parents or friends say about money? Let's face it, if you heard that rich people are assholes, subconsciously there's going to be a natural aversion to you becoming wealthy because subconsciously you don't want to be an asshole. If you think money is the root of all evil, and subconsciously you don't want to be evil, there's going to be a block from you attaining that goal of creating wealth in your life. So, take a minute to gain awareness about any fears or blocks you may have to achieving your desire.

You want to say it out loud. Not only do you want the universe to know what you are trying to manifest, but by voicing it out load it puts the vibration of your intention out to the universe. Plus, you want your partner in manifestation to know what you're manifesting, so a discussion might be in order.

**Step 4** - After saying your intention out loud, give yourself (selves) a few minutes to sit with it and absorb it. Allow yourself (selves) to feel what it would feel like to have it. See what it would look like to have it. Know what it would be like to already have this manifest. Sit in the energy of already having it manifested in your life!

# CHAPTER SEVEN

# Setting up Sacred Space

Let's set up your temple for your sex magic ritual. Setting up sacred space creates an intentional environment for yourself or you and your partner(s). It sets the stage for what's going to occur in the space and creates a container. So, imagine what you would want your space to look like. Do you want to create a special area that invites intimacy? Or use the whole room? Do you want to light some candles, or put some scarves over your lamps to shift the ambiance in the space?

Think about what you may want or need during your time alone or together. Include special objects, stones or crystals, massage oil, lubricant, toys, food and/or drink you may want during, or after.

Begin by clearing your space, you want to clear your space. Sage is a popular energetic cleaning tool. But you can use things native to your culture and your area for cleansing as well. In the Pacific Northwest, cedar and lavender are really popular to use for smudging or simply stating to the universe that your area be cleansed for your highest and best good is enough. I like to say, "Please clear my space of all negative energy. Only good energy and good spirit allowed."

Call in the four directions, if that's a practice of yours. You can also call in your guides, angels, ascended masters, your healing team, or even deities - such as Shiva and Shakti while stating the desire for the space. A simple intention is, "For our highest and best good".

During one of my sacred sex magic sessions, I wanted to see God. So, I set an intention at the beginning of the practice that I wanted to see God. And at the end, in my altered state, I saw Shiva in my internal vision. As I was breathing the energy in and up my central channel after orgasm, I got the image of breathing in the energy Shiva was channeling to me from above as I was seeing Shiva above me channeling his energy into me.

You can invite those deities in to hold sacred space for your ritual, or you can request to embody their energies during your love making process. If you want to be Shiva or Shakti all you need to do is ask to embody them during sexual union. I will add... if you are going to invoke deities, first surround yourself with white light and ask for only the highest and best energies allowed.

This is your sacred space, so you want to create an environment that invites what you desire it to be. Whether that is love, intimacy, sexiness, intuition; does it support your intention?

A great way to do this is with a special altar. It can be as small as a statue, or as elaborate as a center floor piece. Use your imagination and go wild. Put your sacred objects on it, your crystal wands, flowers, crystals, pictures, statues, and anything else that suits your fancy.

Take a minute to think about your sacred space afterwards. You may feel hungry after and it's nice to have something already set up so you can stay in the energy... and not have to leave your sacred space. What kind of food or snacks would you like? Beverages? You can add something for food play, or simply for when you're relaxing, cuddling, and sharing in each other's bliss energy. These invites play, nurturing, and talking about your intentions as well as how you / your partner(s) felt about the experience.

# CHAPTER EIGHT

# Protection

We often hear about people putting themselves in a protective bubble. You may already have this practice for yourself, but let's take it one step further and create one for you and your partner. Here I'd like to share a simple way you and your partner can create a bubble of energetic containment for yourselves within your sacred space.

First, you're going to intend together that you are going to create a sacred bubble to contain your sexual energy to support your sacred union.

## Sacred Bubble Exercise

- Sit facing each other, hands in prayer position at your chest.

- Both of you place your right palms on your partners hearts. Then put your left hands on top of your partners hand that is on your heart.

- Share your intentions with each other. Close your eyes and take a deep centering breath together.

- Now open your eyes and put your hands in prayer position at your chest.

- Lean forward and touch foreheads with closed eyes. This is a tantric kiss. You're making a connection at your sixth chakra. Take a deep breath together and connect.

- Now separate, gazing into each other's eyes and take a breath together. Feel into your connection.

- Now put your palms at chest height facing outward towards your partner, touching each other's palms together in front of yourselves.

- Push your right palm forward and allow your left palm to move back behind your head as your partner presses their right palm forward, thus bicycling your arms, and return back to the starting position with palms together in front of yourselves.

- Now repeat with the other side... pushing your left palm forward past your partners head and allow your right palm to pull back (palms always touching) and bicycling your arms once again... and back to the starting position.

- With palms still together, move both your hands over your partners head, then allow your partners hands to move back over your head (as if to form an infinity pattern when viewed from the side).

- Return your palms to your prayer position at your chest and bow your heads to each other in reverence.

Please see my video available on my YouTube channel, *Raise the Vibe with Liz, titled "Creating a Sacred Bubble."*

# CHAPTER NINE

## Sex Magic Practice

Now we get to the yummy part! You've set up your sacred space, set your intentions and created your sacred bubble... now you can begin to make love in sacred union or solo in a sacred self-pleasure practice.

Sacred sex, or tantric sex, is not to be rushed. Don't rush straight to orgasm! It's not about the end game, getting to climax, or about getting to the finish line. It's about taking your time. Not to mention it takes a woman longer to reach arousal states to be ready for penetration. Again, don't be goal oriented, it's about taking your time to build your energy, your eros. Just allow yourself to follow your pleasure and release any desire to perform. This in itself is a gamechanger, especially for people used to performance and goal-oriented sex.

Yes, you have a goal of manifesting your intention out into the world, but you don't have the goal of orgasm, because what you want to do in sex magic is build your sexual energy up. The more time you can spend doing that, 1-2-3 hours of time, the more energy you build to back your intention when you send it out.

Sacred sex is not only about communing with your partner but also the divine - you are in creation energy. So slow down, don't rush and explore each other. Follow your pleasure!

Invite in all types of touch. Perhaps you begin with a tantric massage to open-up your bodies in a soothing loving way. Or maybe you play with different types of pressure. Play a game where you try touching your partner in different ways and asking them what they like and don't like. Make sweet love to each other, or yourself!

Use edging! Edging is where you build up the sexual tension almost to climax, but you don't orgasm. You let it drop down, then raise it back up, over and over again. Build this energy, then slow it down. Repeat these 3 or 4 times. If you're multi orgasmic that is also building the energy. Experiment, try edging, or build up the sexual energy with touch and breath. Breath moves energy and increases eros. Move the energy with your breath by channeling it up through your body as you're making love, breathing it up into your heart or up through your central channel in practice for release.

When you reach the moment of orgasm, it's time to send those intentions out to the cosmos! World peace!!

Breath the energy from your orgasm at your root, up your body through your chakras, and out the top of your head. While pulling that energy up through your body and shooting it out the top of your head during your entire orgasm... the energy rushes, and the bliss follows. Hold the image of your intention in your mind, visualize it, imagine it, feel it. Feel what it feels like to already have it manifest in your life in the present. See what it looks like to already have it or be it. The universe doesn't know future, the universe knows now. So, imagine, feel, and experience it already alive in your life in this moment.

If your intention is world peace - what would that look like, feel like, be like? Feel what world peace would feel like. See what it would look like. Have an experience of it in your mind. Focus on it. Breathe those surges up through your body.

And keep pulling those up as you get the energetic after waves of energy that go up through your body as well. This is your Kundalini rising-up through the center of your body. Your Kundalini is awakened during orgasm.

Now pull that energy up through the body, work and breath with it. IF you start to tremble or shake, allow it. This is your lifeforce energy. The more you do this, the more you can trigger energetic orgasms as well. And these can last minutes, or sometimes hours after reaching orgasm!

Post orgasm, ride the subtle internal waves, visualize what's going on in your body, feel what's going on in your body and really breath into your bliss. Enjoy it! Not only are you backing your intention, but you're also flooding your body with this energy. You are being fed by your own body with your lifeforce energy.

Now that you've sent the intention and backed it with your eros into the cosmos, release it... Surrender!

You've sent it up and out to spirit to be created into reality. Upon release it's out of your hands. You have now given your ask to the universe for manifestation, and it's now surrendered to divine intervention. By surrendering you let go of the outcome and have faith that the universe will deliver your ask as you have presented it... or better. This or better!

And let's face it, the universe usually has a grander outcome than you could ever imagine. Because the universe has your back and wants you to succeed!

Yes, you can do things in the physical world to help it along and by all means take action.... but release it to source. You've just done all this work. You've backed it with your lifeforce, your energy, sent it out with your partner or solo. So, surrender to the highest and best outcome!

I want to add here that energy travels. If your lover is across the country, you can connect energetically or through the various platforms at your disposal. These days you can not only have phone sex, but you can also have a sex magic date on a video platform. Super sexy!

Your energetic connection can travel across space and time, not to mention the country or the world. You ARE energy, and you are energetically connected, as the energy system is the blueprint of the physical body. Thus, you are an energetic being in a sea of energy that connects all of us across space and time. Your energies will meet even if you're on opposite sides of the planet.

# CHAPTER TEN

## Astral Sex

W^hat is astral sex? Astral sex is the ability to have sex in the ethers. It's having sex on the astral plane using astral projection - a type of out of body experience. It's sex for the soul. Souls travel outside their bodies to another dimension where they're able to have sex. To have an out of body experience with yourself, your partners, deities, or past/future partners. Astral sex is the process of leaving your physical body (at will) behind and intentionally searching out the astral plane. It's a projection of one's consciousness, and the union of conscious experience. The melding of two energies making a connection.

The astral plane is also called the astral realm or the astral world. It's a non-physical realm or level of existence separate from the physical realm. Accessible through the ability of your soul being able to leave your body for a time while staying connected by an etheric cord at our naval.

It's said that the astral realm is where we may find angels, guides, and non-physical beings. You can also do sex magic in the astral realms using the same process I've discussed.

You can induce an out of body experience through techniques such as visualization, breathing and meditation. Start by working with the sensation of your soul separating from your physical body. Once you've become comfortable with that sensation the next step would be traveling to the astral plane once you're comfortable having an out of body experience.

By traveling to the astral plane, you can meet your lover there. You won't need to be physically near each other to do this, of course, as you will be meeting at a soul level. When two souls can transcend their physical bodies and connect on a deeper, more spiritual and intimate level, it can bring them even closer together. It is essentially another type of energetic sex.

Astral sex is also a way we can invite spirit into our sex magic practice. If you would like to make love to Shiva or Shakti, or another Ascended Master, you can invoke them into your practice. If your partner is out of town, you can call in their higher self, or their sexual energy; time and space is an illusion. If you have a deceased loved one, you can call in their sexual energy.

The cosmos is large, and the unseen realms and the layers between worlds are very thin. So, are we able to call in energy from a past, current, or future lover that you haven't even met yet? YES! All you need to do to begin is to imagine it, call it in, then simply let go. Imagine what it would be like for this person to be touching your body, for them to be caressing your body, for them to be penetrating you.

Meet your lover in the cosmos on Indras web, as Buddha called it. Buddha called the web of life Indras web; like we have the World Wide Web. There is an energetic web that goes out beyond us, so you can connect to anything and anyone at any time even if they are across the world. Or you can connect to future lovers you haven't even made love to yet and bring them in. Whether you choose higher beings, past lovers, transcended masters, or meeting your lover in the cosmos, it's all possible.

Bringing in deities isn't an uncommon practice. Tibetan monks practiced karma mudra where they called in deities called Tantrikas or Dakinis. The monks would call to them to help them raise their sexual energy for spiritual liberation, or moksha. Kama Sutra was for pleasure, or the pursuit of pleasure. Karma Mudra is the quest for liberation, for awakening, so they would call in the deity to have sex with them to raise their sexual energy to be able to manifest it.

Protection is important! Before you journey beyond the veil, take a moment to create a sacred container of light. Close your eyes and visualize an orb of white energy at your heart center. With each breath, allow this light to expand - filling your body, then your aura, then the space around you until you are completely surrounded in a brilliant white sphere of protection.

Silently affirm: "I am safe, I am sovereign, I am protected. Only energies of love and light may enter my space." Feel the vibration settle, like a soft hum wrapping you in calm certainty. From within this sanctuary, your spirit may travel freely; held, protected, and in perfect alignment with your highest good.

# CHAPTER ELEVEN

# Daily Pleasure Practice

I recommend a daily pleasure practice for everyone. Having a pleasure practice has many benefits, especially if you're working with your energy or if you're working with your Kundalini energy. To awaken kundalini, work on that self-pleasure!

It really helps open you up and not only do you learn about your body (what you like and what you don't like) but when you're having partnered sex, you can share with your partner what you like and don't like. It's a great practice to start opening that 5th chakra at your throat and learning to have a voice for your pleasure. A simple – "Hey, I was experimenting the other day and I'd really like you to do THIS to me." And how sexy that will sound to your partner hearing about what brings you pleasure. Plus, no guessing on their part anymore!

Use your imagination and get curious with your body. This is your temple. Create sacred time for yourself. Give yourself a massage with some massage oil and take it slow, just like you would during partnered sex... it's an act of self-love. Massage your breasts, your arms, your belly, and your legs before moving on to your yoni (vulva). Communicate and listen to your body. Ask your yoni if she's ready to be touched or penetrated. How often are we asked if our vulvas are ready to be touched or penetrated? Spend some time getting to know your yoni and explore in the way that brings you the most pleasure. Ladies, if you've not yet seen your vulva, get a mirror out and look at her! Get to know her and her beauty.

This daily pleasure practice is just as important for male bodies as female bodies, despite the verbiage used in the example being predominantly female.

Really charge up your own personal energy, not just going straight for that orgasm. Because so often you're taught the end game - that orgasm is the goal. You're taught to get it over with fast. Perhaps as a youth you were worried your friends or siblings would catch you. Or if mom was coming down the hall, you need to be able to cum quickly. Or that you should stroke yourself quickly instead of taking your time. Or even pound it like you saw on porn. Ladies and gentlemen, here's your chance to breathe and to enjoy yourself just for the pleasure of it!

Undo those programs from the past and create new neural pathways for your pleasure... because you can still have those ideas in the back of your head that somebody's going to open that door and see you. So really allow yourself the time to get to know yourself. To just experience your pleasure. Ease your nervous system around pleasure and re-write your inner book; allow yourself to spend this quality time with yourself.

Practice building up your eros energy so when you do have that orgasm during sex magic you experience all that it has to offer... you have your pleasure, you have the ecstatic energy to back your magic, and you can have that mind blowing powerful orgasm you've been craving (on your own or partnered) and beyond that... into multiple orgasms, energetic orgasms, and everlasting cosmic orgasms!

# CHAPTER TWELVE

# Let's Get Witchy

If you want to get a little witchy with your sex magic, you can add various things to your space or process. After writing down your intentions, put them under your mattress and leave them there.

Say you're solo and you're looking for love... you can write down everything that you want in a partner on a piece of paper, fold it and stick it under the mattress as your main intention. Maybe draw a heart around it to emphasize what you desire.

You can introduce color into your sex magic practice. The chakra colors are a good way to do that. If you are wanting to bring in money, think first chakra and use red, or of course green, because green is the color of money.

If you are manifesting love, try using pink for a compassionate lover, or red for a passionate love. Use colored markers to write out your intentions. Grab some colored candles, yellow for personal power, blue to speak clearly or purple to strengthen intuition.

You can also charge the toys you're going to bring into your sex magic sacred space under the full moon. The full moon is really a great time for clearing and charging, especially if you're including things like your crystal wand, crystal yoni egg, or your yoni wand. Crystals love a salt bath or smudging for cleansing, or to be set out in a moon bath. And it's also a great way to charge them up before bringing them into your sexual practice.

Speaking of the moon, the full moon and new moon are great times for sex magic. If you're trying to release something, I would recommend the New Moon. But if you're trying to manifest something then use the Full Moon. Some magicians bring in their moon blood for added potency.

Ladies, if you're on your bleed and you collect your moon blood, it can boost the potential of your magic when you put it on the altar since it increases the energy. You can even be bold and anoint yourself with it...

And use your intuition! What comes to your mind that you would want to bring into your sacred space? What would help you change your energy body, your Ka body, like they do in Isis temple arts in Egypt? What's coming to mind that you would like in your space that will help you increase your sexual energy? The possibilities are endless!

## *Remember your...*

- Mind - Establishes the Intention
- Body - Produces the Fuel
- Soul - Puts it in Motion
- Spirit - Oversees the Result

### *The Sex Magic Practice:*

- You are grounded, centered, and integrated.

- You have cleared and set up your space.

- You have set your intention.

- You have run your eros and channeled it through your body creating the fuel to back your intention.

- You have released it out into the cosmos to the divine via your orgasm.

- The divine puts your intention into motion and oversees the result.

*IT IS MANIFEST!*

# About the Author

Aseer, seeker, and spiritual explorer, Liz Peterson is an intuitive energy healer, Reiki Master, spiritual coach, oracle reader, and podcaster. Liz has been a lifelong student of healing, personal growth, and metaphysics. She is the host of the podcast Raise the Vibe with Liz: dedicated to bringing today's psychics, healers, way-showers, inspirational speakers, and ascension leaders to an international audience. Her podcast mission is to heal the world, one guest at a time.

A mother of 4, Liz lives on a small island in the Pacific Northwest where she enjoys all life has to offer. She uses her natural born abilities, and her personal journey of healing, transformation, and empowerment in her work with individuals. With love and compassion, it's her personal mission to assist others on their spiritual journey of awakening and healing. Liz empowers and guides people to clear and release stuck energy, blocks and trauma while activating the body's natural healing process. You can find her offerings on - *www.raisethevibewithliz.com*

www.ingramcontent.com/pod-product-compliance
Lightning Source LLC
Chambersburg PA
CBHW030508130626
46549CB00007B/2893